This Beckoning Ceaseless Beauty

Also by Heidi Rose Robbins:

Sanctuary

THIS

BECKONING
CEASELESS
BEAUTY

Heidi Rose Robbins

First Published in 2013
by Radiant Life Publishing

Copyright © 2013 by Heidi Rose Robbins

ISBN: 978-0-9910789-0-5

This book is dedicated to
my loves,
Andrew
Kate
and Dylan.

Table of Contents

Thresholds

Ripening

Come In

Saving Graces

| THRESHOLDS |

O n e

One (intimate) glance
can open something
long closed within us.

One (full) breath
can ease
an ancient fear.

One (tender) touch
can soothe
unspeakable pain.

One (loving) word
can soften
an armored heart.

One (radical) thought
can spark
unfathomable daring.

One (courageous) step
can change forever
the course of a life.

Morning Walk

Frost kisses the oranges.
Curious with cold, the birds
chatter amongst themselves.
I walk briskly down a stretch
of road looking for patches of sun.

My hands
plunged in pockets,
my brow crinkled
with morning plans.

She rides towards me
on a rickety blue bike
weaving back and forth
to make the incline easier.

Her hair silver and flowing,
she is flushed
like a child who has come
to report her latest adventure.

Her face,
open, fresh, smooth,
like a saint really
who carries only love.

Even with the effort of the climb,
delight ripples in her wake.

When we meet,
her eyes shine.
She laughs,
"Wait till you see the snow!"

She might have said,
Wait till you see beauty everywhere.
Wait till you know the secret of all things.
Wait till you know you are love.

But she says what she does and rides by,
her story told,
her message delivered.

I look to the capped peak
in the distance.
I see the beauty of a mountain
rarely covered in winter,
while my body is melting into spring.
Tears stream down my face.
A hardness around my heart,
dissolves.

I fling open my arms
and gather her goodness
to my chest
as my body breaks into blossom.

"What till you see the snow,"
I whisper,
"Wait till you see it,"
her unabashed love
careening,
ricocheting
through my now
vast heart.

Nothing But Itself

The heart,
you know,
left to its own devices,
has no edges,
or walls,
no limits,
no borders,
no stop signs,
no crinkly bits,
no grudges,
nothing frozen,
nothing numb,
nothing broken.

It is heat and light,
blazingly generous,
pulsing with the power of
ten thousand suns.

This morning I felt shy.
Instead of beating myself
up about it,
I noticed what my heart wanted
right then, which was
simply this:
To be itself.

Open, limitless, raw,
fierce, magnificent, tender,
solar, boundless, radiant.

So, I thought, why not?
I unfurled my chest,
smiled at my shyness
and let my heart
do its thing.

Let Me Say it Straight

You can't write a poem
if you can't feel your heart.

I would argue
it isn't worth reading one
if your heart
is otherwise occupied.

I'm not saying a thing
about the state of the vessel.
Bring it broken,
guarded or heavy.
Bring the yearning,
the ache,
the celebration.

But bring it.

It's beating under
everything
after all.

Don't allow the escape
to regions north of the neck.
You've seen that vista before.

I'm begging you to travel
to the fiery center,
not suspend above it.

Let me say it straight.
I want the heart of the matter,
even if it means
a good bushwhack
through guarded,
precarious terrain.

Uncommonly Low

If we meet this afternoon
in an elevator
on the way to the 22nd floor
and you smile and
happen to ask,

"How are you?"

If I dare speak the truth
I would say:

"I am uncommonly low,
my friend.
Low like a reptile,
barely moving,
hardly breathing,
shifty-eyed low."

At which point you might
grow silent or shake your head
or say, "Sorry to hear that."

And I would, of course, understand.
Saying something like that
makes everyone uncomfortable.

But what if you said,
"Honey. Child. I know,"
and reached out to hug me,
and I just fell into your arms.
What if we just kept hugging even through
all the announcing-the-22nd-floor-dings.

What if the doors opened and
someone got on and tried to ignore us,
but we started laughing and crying
at the same time

and that someone joined in because
she knew a seismic shift was underway
and it looked like huge relief
with all that weight and sadness and fatigue
flinging down the elevator shaft.

Then what if we all just sat
on the elevator floor and rode it up and down
like I did once in college greeting everyone
with a giddy hello, forgetting everything
but the sweetness of an unpredictable ride.

Whole-Hearted

I am today
full of my

Self.

Oh glorious day.

Today is not
for fierce mother love,
lover's embrace,
or circles of friends
held with strong arms.

Today,
I am solitary.
I have sanctuary.
I am sovereign,
queen of my time.

Oh extravagant day.

I am bursting at the seams of constraint,
overflowing with expectation,
offering whole-heartedly
the brilliant
radiant
unfolding soul.

I have found my place
today
in the ongoing
exaltation and celebration
underlying everything.

Today my heart knows no bounds.

All fatigue is
answered not
with fullness of sleep
but fullness of
Self.

I'm Planting a Garden

I who have managed
to let die
most every green thing
to cross my path,
am planting a garden.

I'll admit
I may be starving
for the metaphor.

But let's just say
I'm hungry for lush green,
ripe goodness,
and plenty of it.

I'm surely not aware
what it will take
but will share with you now
what I do know
so we are all certain
I gave it my best shot.

I imagine it must go something
like this:

Choose good ground,
ground that invites you.
Even if it appears empty
know full well it is not,
nor ever has been.

Soften the soil.
Mix it up.
Let it run through your fingers.
Give that earth some air
so it welcomes what you wish to plant.

I was going to say
plant the seed.
But already--
I'm getting ahead of myself.

Choose it first.
Choose with care.
You can scatter random seeds without thought,
but that's not the garden you're planting now.

What bounty is your whole body yearning
to receive?
Choose it.
Remember that sometimes it looks like
what it will become and sometimes not.

Then, yes,
plant it.
Plant the tiny seed.
Note that you won't ever see that
seed again in such a potent form.
Trust enough to let the ground swallow it.

Cover it up
with a wish.
Or a prayer.
Or your fingers crossed.
Pat it with firm hands.
Acknowledge the sun and welcome it.
Moisten the earth with a hose or tears
or dance the dance of rain.

And then wait.
And listen.
And listen.
And wait.

Keep it company with a song
or children playing in the sprinkler,
with hammock Sundays,
with a few good poems.

Listen, just for kicks,
for the seed cracking open,
feel for the texture of life unfolding,
try to catch the uncatchable moment
when green bursts through silent earth.

And then can you do this?

Welcome innocence.
Welcome fragility.
Welcome awe.

Don't know what to do.
But do it anyway.

Guard growth like a fierce mama bear.
Avoid excessive exposure to unrelenting heat.
Offer shade with the fullness of your quiet body.
Avoid deluge.
Nourish with drops.

Wait and listen.
Wait and listen.
Because here's where it's easy to blow it.

Don't get distracted with the full, fecund
farmer's market basket of plenty
spilling out endless bounty
ready for consumption.

Just be curious about your babies,
curious in a way those that lift us most
ask us questions,
questions that touch the seedling
of our strength and allow it to sing to the sun.

I'd say absolutely
expect blossoming,
outrageous blossoming,
all in good time.

But remember the
all
in
good
time
part.

Time is good.
It grows things.
It grows us.
It does not run out
but runs with us
whispering

Now...
Now...
Now...

Have you heard time's song?
He is singing to you now.
He is not counting hours.
He is singing to you.

And even when the seedling,
life insisting on life,
stretches to a fullness
in which most who see it say
"Well, look at you. So glorious.
So bright. So full. How did you do it?
How are you doing it? Just keep it up, up, up."

Don't go there.
Run with time freely and joyously.
Breathe in these moments
of strength.
Don't draw any conclusions.
Don't get distracted.
Don't assume that now is the time
to push for the prize.

Now is the time
to sit with the growing beauty.
To sit still, not knowing.
To sit, still not knowing.

Water and listen.
Water and listen.

Do the work,
the practice,
of yanking the cut throat weeds
that grow swiftly and without care.

Because you care.
You care deeply.
But show this in the daily hours of living
not in every moment's fret.

Feed what is growing.
Walk in sunlight.
Notice the breath that moves in and
the breath that is released.

And then,
And now,

Wake up
one morning,
dear one,
and run out of doors.
There, on this day when you
expect it least,
you will find yourself
standing in a garden
of your own allowing.

Your work,
your love,
your daily necessities,
all woven inseparably
into every thriving thing.

And your blossom,
dear love,
full, lavish, distinct.

| RIPENING |

Stuck in Sad Time

To begin,
I am sad.
It is a small sorrow
in a great world
but fills
this moment
entirely.

Do not tell a soul.
This sadness
can be carried
quietly.

I will cry
as I walk
to the dry cleaners
carrying my favorite
hopelessly stained
dress.

I am good at my life.
Can't you tell?
I am pleasant.
You are pleased.

No one need know
I sit
stunned
on the couch
for hours.

I want to strip,
smear my face,
Open my mouth,
pour sweet wine,
too much,

over my face, my breasts,
down
my throat.

I want to dance
for leering men,
turn my back
leave them starving.

I want
to be
too much,
not enough,
never
just right.

I want to undo
any precious peace,
unravel my careful life,
uproot
the lily.

I want
to break
something
perfect.

I do not
wish to sit
on the couch
so far away
from any life
I'm meant
to live.

I am stuck
in sad time

where everything
is just
out of reach.

I'm not blind.
Even here
there are
sweet fields
of red blood
poppies.

Even here
there are
hot springs bubbling
from the Earth.

I will roll
in that blushing quilt,
soak in lapping heat.

But first,
I will stand.
I will walk
to the dry cleaners,
pick up my dress.

It will
still
be stained.

I will hold it
high
so it does not
drag
on the long
walk
home.

Sugar Baby

I want to be sugar in the raw,
sweet enough to change the taste of things.
I want to be sugar in the raw for my lover.
Soft. Bountiful. A bowl full of me.

I don't want to be hiding out, sipping life.
I want to be innocent, unprotected.
Raw sugar.
Sugar baby.
I want to be wanted, tasted, licked,
held close until it's time for the yum.

My lover treats me like I am.
For him, I am the only sugar around.
I may be hard as salt water taffy,
needing to be chewed and kneaded and worked
before the prize.
I may be lemony and sour and sharp on his tongue
before he works to the smooth sweetness.
But I'm his sugar.

Oh sugar child,
Oh sugar mama,
Oh baby, baby, baby.
I'm talking to myself now. I full-bodied know
the sweetness I am and want to give into it just a little,
so that I soften like caramel and spread that richness
for myself and anyone who wants a taste.

Too much? I hope so. It's no vow broken.
It's just warm and revealed and flush and available.
It's me, daring to be the deliciousness of life,
not standing outside of it growing gray,
not crumpling in with the weight,
not limiting the freedom of the fullest, juiciest offering.

Because baby. Because sugar.
The sweetness of life is real.
I am tired of looking through the candy store window.
I want to press my face against the glass,
feel its cool hard smoothness,
eye every sweet thing and then walk through the door and roll in it.
I want to shed every bit of gray,
color my body with sweetness, tootsie pop,
dip my hands into every soft colored powder and suck.
Because I am tired of a pinched, drawn face
and the weight I carry.

Call me cotton candy. Call me sugar love.
Call me raw. But call me.
I want to be called and consumed and asked to give it all.
Sugar love, know this: I'm good chocolate.
I'm silky and smooth and my taste lingers.
I've just been a little shy and a pinch preoccupied.
It's taken a life time of playing Candy Land
to remember that every spot is sweet on the way
and there's nothing to do but give into it.
Sugar. Sugar. Love.

Being all grown up doesn't leave room
for the daily trip to the Stop 'n Go with a quarter in my pocket.
I'm spending now, and I'm choosing carefully,
a wide variety of YUM,
because I've been hungry for too long.

But guess what, Dreamsicle. I'm the candy too.
Every bite I take of sweetness,
I'm licked by love like a mama cat.
Sugar, I want to be soft and willing and ready.
And I am. Sugar love. I am.

Home

When it was done,
when words were spoken that cannot be unsaid,
the silence kissed my eyes and mouth
and whispered into the caves of my heart.

All my life
I heard the joyous music
in a village just around the bend.
Though the music was
wild, and free and insistent,
and though my heart
stirred from the strains I could dimly hear,
I never chose to go.

There was work to be done
after all.

But after all
when there was nothing left to do
but walk
in the last blazes of the sun
from all that was familiar

I opened my eyes
freshly kissed
and in wordless wonder
followed this
beckoning, ceaseless beauty
Home.

I Want to Tell You

I want to tell you that I speak of light
because my body often
feels like a hard, knotted thing,

I sing of love
because caution caught in my throat
thirty years ago and I'm still trying to
spit it out.

I want to tell you
I feel raw
when I speak what is
closest to my heart,
that I look for a jaded disguise,
that who I love, what I love and how I love
make me tremble.

I want to tell you
that some days
I wear darkness like a cool leather jacket,
feel its weight, its protection, its belonging.

But more days, I want to strip,
letting illusion fall around my feet
and stand witnessed as a body.

I want to tell you that I am tired,
but I am willing.

I want to tell you that sometimes
the right words
scrawled on a page
save my life.

Fire Moves Fast Across the Valley

My room at the Inn is for lovers.
There's a bed bigger than a small pond,
a tub with clawed feet,
a balcony with two chairs
nestled together.

Far from lonely,
I am expectant.

I sit outside in dappled light,
pen in hand, listening.
Gusts of wind spill seed-pods on my lap.
The trees are whispering.

They know my silent invitation.

My stillness,
My quiet breath
belie my invocation.

But rest is required for
surrender to flame.

The beauty of the day,
unbearable.
My skin is thinning.

Oh my loves.
Can I tell you I am curious?

Already I am burning.
Everything is.
The dance around the flame is done.

It is time,
(as there always is a time)
as cycles end,

as planets move,
to stand at the center
and burn.

And yes,
now the wind has left the trees,
do you hear?

Fire moves fast across the valley.

There is nothing to be lost--
fear devoured, yes,
dark obstruction turned to ash.

And yes, the heat.
And yes, the letting go.
And yes.
And yes.
And yes.

I Who Love Mountains and All They Signify

I who love mountains and all they signify
find sanctuary in valleys,
where quiet truths are
echoed back
from mountain sides.

I ask a question
and reflection
careens off
sides of earth
allowing my breath to steady
and body to calm.

Here in the valley
closer to the beat
of the heart
of the earth,
I hear the essential.

I who love mountains and all they signify
choose here
to lay the earth of my body
on the body of the earth
in this sanctuary of silence.

And only
only
only
in this deep surrender
is the scent
of a great ascent
yet to come.

Morning Light

The early hour.
The scent of something past.
The growing light in the sky.
The wisp of cloud.
The crispness of morning.
The ripening of the orange grove.
The chisel of mountain top.
The rawness of my heart.
The whisper of the possible.
The stillness that softens.
The new face in the mirror.

What to Do with Sadness

When sadness lingers,
When loneliness creeps in to sit beside you
And will not leave,
When you can no longer feel a spark of joy
In even a hidden corner,

Find something,
Anything
That is burning--
A star
A porch lamp
A candle on the table.

Then, imagine that light
At the center of your heart
And remember
You are molten love.

The only thing to do
With sadness
Is to introduce it to
Indestructible Beauty--
To the flame
Of love
Present in every
Living thing.

Start with a
Morning glory
Or a sparrow.
Start with the
Spirited eyes
Of the woman
Who serves you
Coffee.
Start with a poem.

Say,
Sadness meet cherry blossom.
Despair meet the Ninth Symphony.
Grief meet the eyes of a child.

Then,
Be very, very quiet,
And let them converse for a time.

Nameless

We are not who we say we are.
There are no words for that name,
none full enough.
Our name is a symphony,
a sunrise.
It is a name that holds all the
sounds of silence.

We are not who we say we are
though we insist it is so.

Maybe we should listen for the name
the sky has to offer,
or the redwood.
It would be loving and infinitely simple.

Let's lay each name
we've spoken
into a greater flame.

Let's soften the grasp
on what is only ours
and breathe the terror,
the flush of freedom.

Let's be nameless
for a time
and listen.

|COME IN|

Always Wave to Airplanes

"Always wave to airplanes,"
you say
as we lay atop
a grassy hill
and try to whistle
through thick pieces of grass
pressed between our thumbs.

You brush the hair
from my forehead
and trace in my palm
letters spelling love.

"Maybe they see us,"
you say.
"Maybe they'll tip their wing,
say hello."

We wave and holler
at the plane just above us,
reaching out to touch
its metal belly,
then plug our ears
from engine's roar.

I wave back,
the pilot now.
I see us far below
sprawled
like newlyweds
on autumn grass.

I wish us well.

At Last

He picks me up,
my body of angles,
to bed,
grasps my back
molds it
into an arch of yearning.

The breath he takes for me
reminds me.
His hands
press into resistance
opening an insistent bud.

Each petal he unfolds
leaves me more naked.
Only his eyes touch my skin.

All I know now,
mouth on breast
hand on belly
thigh on hip.

My body,
at last,
come in.
Come in.

Last Night

Last night,
my love,
is only ours.

Your impress
now forever in
my breath
moves with and through me.

Something long silent,
speaks as my body unfurls
in your care.

Love,
You lift and carry
my wild, fragile,
searching self
and with your
listening touch,
vanquish
doubt, apology, shame.

You ask only
that I revel in receiving.

Oh
how you
grow me
in your love.

Undiscovered Country

I did not know
the rushing river,
its endless curves,
playful eddies.

There is a spot
just off my hip
where you found it.

I've always known
the great plains,
the weather obvious for miles,
the trail unerringly straight.

Now your hand
brushes my breast
uncovers virgin landscapes
wild with blossoming.

One hundred monarchs
fly simultaneously
from the lone tree
of my belly.

You are charting
my unknown country.

Even alone now
I can hear water
splashing rock.

The Kiss of Sky

I sit in a rusty white chair
at the center of a grassy field.

The green lushness of mountain before me
cuts into unceasing blue.

I breathe
to stand with the row of trees
that line the highest ridge.
We offer ourselves
to light's kiss
unfurling to receive the gift of sky.

Here I see why we must
fall to our knees
in our greatest moments of victory.

At the summit
there are no words
to name the infinite.
All we achieve must melt
into awe.

Here at the threshold of
ancient earth and boundless sky
we have this:
Our tender body.
Our breath.
Our beating heart.

And our yearning,
our deepest yearning
to be touched,
to be kissed
by limitless
love.

Renewal

I'm driving with my family
through Gallup, New Mexico.
The ninth grade is holding a car wash
in the high school parking lot.
They stand with signs,
half awkward in apology,
half in sheer delight
wholly in love.

Something in the way one body
pushes against another
stops my breath,
hurtling me back through years
to some joy
my body has never forgotten.

I turn my face to the window,
tears impossible to explain,

except to say
time unfolds in unexpected ways
and the linear isn't most true.

Every part of me
is young and expectant,
curious and full, shy and
in love, in love, in love.

Even tonight
in the darkness,
wrapped in my husband's arms,
the children asleep,

My body sings.

SAVING GRACES

Write a Poem

I am listless
in the living room.
The hours stretch until bed,
an interstate on a huge fold-out map.

The kids are wrestling.
My husband has a deadline.
I am unhinged,
morose,
ripe with self-criticism.

As half joke, half plea
I say to my husband,
"I need some masculine guidance."

"Write a poem,"
he says.
"You have fifteen minutes.
I'm starting the timer now.
Go."

I didn't really expect an answer.
He shoos me to the bedroom,
as I grab my book and ball point,
closes the door.

I sit in the blue chair
we've had since Kate was born.
It's covered in socks with no mates,
a swim suit,
and the jeans I wore yesterday.
The bed is unmade.

I open my book,
write three words, scratch them out,
look out the window.

Now the kids are taking a bath.
My husband washes the dishes.
Dylan calls for me but his need is quickly answered.
There's some laughter,
splashing in the tub.

I should help dry the dishes,
get the kids in pajamas,
clean this room.

I start again.
A new page.
A few lines this time.

Now Kate is playing the piano.
Dylan is brushing his teeth.
Andrew is drying dishes.
They all seem to be singing
to one another
far away
but oh so close.

I feel good
quite suddenly
nestled in the thick of things,
scribbling on the page.

"Time's up,"
my husband calls,
an end if I want one.
But I don't.

Their voices touch my pen,
and I am falling into
some kind of wholeness.

I look at my hand, my wrist,
my lungs expanding.
I see my pen on the page,
a page now full.
I feel the contours of my body,
my very grateful body,
come gently
into focus.

Grand Canyon

When you are six months in my belly,
your father and I travel to the Grand Canyon.
In all my 36 years I've never been.
You have to see it, your father says, it will change you.
We stop on our way back from Boulder, Colorado.
We want to celebrate our fourth anniversary amidst beauty.

I cannot speak when I first glimpse
the canyon lines through the trees.
It opens every closed place inside me.
I gulp the redness of the rock like one dying of thirst.
Your father watches and smiles.
He knows I am fed by majesty.
The redwoods left me silent and full for weeks.

The road ends at our hotel.
We drop our bags in a spare clean room
and without pause leave to walk the canyon's edge.
Hand in hand, we climb to rocks that hang suspended
above everything and nothing.
We sit and rest and kiss and stare.
We take pictures of condors flying overhead,
unable to believe their size, the span of wing.

That night your father cajoles a reluctant host
to give us a reservation that does not exist
to dine by a window at dusk and watch the canyon disappear.
We make love that night, my round belly between us
and fall asleep curled tightly in one another's arms.

The alarm rings at 4 am.
Still groggy with sleep, we dress without a word.
We drive 10 minutes, park and two doors slam.
Stepping through the trees we find others waiting.
We choose a quiet place to watch the return of the sun.
You stir in my belly.

There is silence as the lines of the canyon sharpen.
I open my arms to the breaking rays of dawn.
The first light floods your home with beauty.

Here there is no fear--I breathe in.
Here I let go--I breathe out.
Here the canyon's walls hold all I can release.
I stretch my arms still further
to wrap them around this timeless moment.
Your father steps back to quietly take a picture.

One year later you are in my arms,
your beauty as exquisite as the canyon at dawn.
This morning, the picture your father took slips from my journal.
As I hold it so we both can see, you pat the picture
with your chubby, precious baby hands.

I imagine it in those hands years from now.
You've found it while reading the stories of my young life.
You study it knowing you too are there.
You wonder if I am happy.
You wonder if I am afraid.
You wonder if my arms are outstretched
in embrace or surrender or both.
You exhale.
Over time, over distance, through silence,
I rush back to hold you
as you open your own arms
to release all you need not carry
and embrace all that's yet to come.

Why Look Forward

It is Tuesday afternoon
on a perfect spring day.
My husband carries
our baby daughter
on a circular mown path
around a meadow.
He lifts her to his shoulders,
disappearing for a moment
behind a tree.
They walk through
a patch of shade
and out again.

I imagine he is singing to her
or naming the flowers and birds
in the field.

She is surely laughing.
Her perfect head
bobs up and down
through dappled light.

They could hear me if I called.
I stand and watch on the steps
of our cabin.
We are here to celebrate
five years of marriage.

When first we came
we were newlyweds.
Now we arrive with
new life.

Soon they will return
to me,
to this little home.
Their journey will end.
Tomorrow will come.

Why look forward?
Why desire anything but this?
Why long for a moment other than now?

For now,
here now,
are flowers and sunlight,
my husband, child and I
inseparably dancing
in a meadow
awash with
love.

Send Mama Chocolate

Here's my advice:
Send your mama chocolate.

Because when she calls to thank you
for the twelve chocolate bars on her doorstep,
her little girl self will be all you hear.
You will forget
who is mama and who is daughter.
You'll swim in a sea of her delight.

A moment like this
must not be taken lightly.
It lifts you
imperceptibly off the sidewalk
for a solid
joyous hour.

While you walk aloft
note your new respect for anything
that carries your love so simply.

I promise you this.
Once you taste this sweetness,
there's no turning back.
You'll send chocolate more often,
or something equally delicious.
Now that it made your mama so happy.

The Littlest Conductor

I carry you before me
into a spring morning.
You sit upright
in a blue fabric pouch,
the littlest conductor
of a Hallelujah chorus.
Your hands
meet and clasp,
dance and point.
You hear what we cannot,
the song in every living thing.

You cannot help but giggle.
Your little hands call forth
the unexpected song
in all who pass.
Their own delight
lifts them
for an unnoticed moment
off the sidewalk,
then returns them
to the ground
with a caught breath,
an unplanned smile.

You raise your hands
far above your head
insisting the final exquisite notes
awake even the most tired of hearts.
Then, without ado
you lay your head
in your tiny hands
on the soft edge of your pouch
and fall asleep.

Around the Table

My husband
wants a family dinner
with substance.

"Let's go around the table
and say three things
we're thankful for."

My son,
four and buoyant,
marches
around the table.

"Love," he says.
"Family," he says.
"Trucks!"
He sits as punctuation.

My daughter giggles.
 "Why did you just walk
around the table?"

"Daddy said," my son replies.

I realize just as my husband does.
We laugh.
We can't stop.
My son beams.
He knows he's done something
wonderful.

And I am grateful
three times over

for this tiny
shining
moment.

P r a y e r

The prayer we say,
my daughter and I,

the prayer we say at night,
that welcomes
the angels and fairies,
thanks them for
protecting and loving us,

that prayer
invites
my daughter's
own private angel,
the one that has been
with her since the beginning,
the one that will always be with her.

Everything
is unknown
except that she walks
in the light of her
very own angel.

And she can't
get too lost
or bewildered
or lonely
if she knows that.

For Elizabeth, Who Walks in Brooklyn

Not just Brooklyn
but Denver and Dallas,
Concord and Aspen,
Athens.

She walks where she finds herself.
Every day.
She walks with a good pace
on strong legs,
a hearty spirit.

Some days
she leaves behind
a small sadness
or a full out bloody battle.

Most days
she walks with joy,
her good cheer
shining outward
waking all that
cross her path.

She changes her life daily
as she walks,
grace and ferocity
alive in every step.

She is my walking friend
marching forward
in spite of anything,
in spite of everything,
she walks.

Her walk says,
"there is power in each step
that later we call our journey."

Her steps call out
'Beauty and Strength.
Beauty and Strength.
Beauty and Strength.'

Oh my walking friend,
there is goodness
in your wake.

Christmas

Mom plants
a bulb
in moist dirt.
A gift
for my older brother,
Brennon.
Her hands press
the dark earth into the
white pot.

"You can watch it
grow each day."

Brennon places it
on the empty window sill.
Perhaps it will sprout
while he is away.

He lives alone.
We have come
to take him
home for Christmas.

We stay in
his spare
clean rooms
only long enough
to plant
the bulb.

Mom brushes
the dirt off
onto her jeans.
She leaves
the white hope
of Amaryllis
for her eldest son.

Ecstasy and a Cabin Mouse

There's a mouse caught in the heating unit.
I don't know much about heaters but I'm here
in this little rustic cabin and it's attached to the wall.
There's a metal pipe, a vent of sorts, that leads outside.
But this mouse is stuck somewhere I can't reach.

Every few minutes, the scrape of little feet fills the silence.
I'm imagining him trying to climb some smooth, vertical surface
and failing repeatedly. His attempts are further apart now and
I'm feeling helpless.

Jim, a man of many gifts who works this land, came yesterday
and put a rope down the vent so the mouse might crawl out,
get some traction, chew his way up even. Clearly it isn't
working.

This morning in yoga, I struggled to stay in an asana that was
impossibly difficult. My beloved teacher happened to be standing
near and took that moment to remind us that our relationship
to this pose was equivalent to our capacity to experience ecstasy.
I burst into tears.

It made a perfect sad sense to me. My hard working, responsible,
duty bound self choked and sputtered, laughed and sobbed.

I hope that little mouse realizes there's a way out, even if it takes some
work. There's a whole ecstatic wilderness out there.

2.

My mouse keeps scratching. I'm thinking no matter how hard he works
he may not be able to crawl out of his confinement. Some force
greater than his valiant attempts is needed now. I may be that force.

I'm also beginning to think my mouse is a chipmunk and though I'm ashamed to admit it, I'm feeling even more urgency to get him out. Two chipmunks are standing vigil outside the heating vent. One keeps leaping on the screen and pressing herself against it, willing it to give way.

I leave messages everywhere, knock on doors, and finally find a wrench to yank this thing off the wall. But there's gas involved and stripped screws and I am not that handy. I give up on the tools and instead assure the chipmunk that I'm working on it.

I'm not sure I've experienced a knight in shining armor but when Jim appears with his tool belt, I practically kiss him. I pace as he works. When he's ready we both pull the unit from the wall. Nothing. We carry it out to the grass and tilt it on its side, propping it up with a log and a rock. Nothing. Then, the scurry of feet. I sit watching the exit pipe.

Then, plop. The cutest little chipmunk, birthed into the light of day, stands, blinks, and scurries off. I clap. I sigh. I practically dance. Just as I begin to thank Jim, we hear more scratching. He smiles. I listen. Giddy now, I watch again. Plop. Another little one blinks and bolts. Two! Jim gets up to pack his tools and a third emerges. Then his sibling follows. Four. Four free baby chipmunks.

I am crying, jubilant, ecstatic.

CPSIA information can be obtained at www.ICGtesting.com
Printed in the USA
BVOW03*1159220814

363648BV00001B/6/P